To Christopher – an unexpectedly
fully - immersed h
um)

U — U
1/5/20 24

Gardening Gaffes

or

*Unintended Consequences
leading to Horticultural Horrors*

Jeremy Hornsby © 2020

Illustrations by Jane Jackson © 2020

A Deebee Publication © 2020
ISBN 978-1-5272-6383-3

Designed and printed by Orbitpress Ltd
www.orbitpress.co.uk

For Jay, an assiduous gardener

Herschel Fitzappleby

Herschel Fitzappleby thought growing onions
Could be the ultimate cure for his bunions,
Seeing those bulbs as a wonderful treat
For the repair of his suffering feet.
But, when he sliced them to end all his cares,
None were surprised it all ended in tears.

Elijah Hopkins

Elijah Hopkins swore he'd seen
The nation's fastest runner bean;
He trained it with terrific style
To run in the Olympic mile;
But when the bean would not comply,
Elijah ate it in a pie.

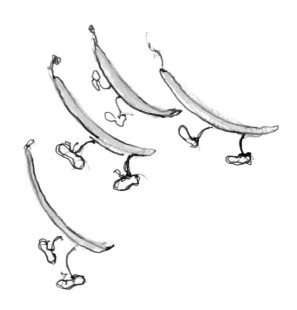

Sir Jeremiah Thimble thought
He'd plant ten pumpkins for some sport
At Hallowe'en; he'd cut some faces,
Making them smile in various places;
Guess his despair when his eyes fell on
One very disappointing melon.

Hugh Bingleter declared "I can't
Succeed with any kind of plant.
I've watered them and fed them well,
But plants and I don't seem to gel."
So now Hugh's garden looks fantastic,
With blooms of multi-coloured plastic.

Percival Bagshotte caused quite a stir
When he replaced his old oak with a fir.
He could detect, he declared, in his bones,
That a great future resided in cones;
How disappointed he was, when he found
Fir cones were selling for fifty a pound.

It occurred to Sir Elkington Rissles
To protect his redcurrants with thistles,
Which his wife by mistake
Then installed in a cake,
Thus reducing his voice to some whistles.

Little Miss Trumpington

Little Miss Trumpington wanted to know
How high the flowers in her garden would grow;
All the long summer she thought them a failure,
Till she was wholly eclipsed by a dahlia;
Going to prove, if a moral you need,
No-one should ever disparage a seed.

Captain Sir Donald Swordfish dreamt
That lest his garden be unkempt
The major thing a groundsman needs
Is loads of stuff to kill the weeds,
And bucketfuls of poisoned plugs
To deal with all the snails and slugs.
Then, with a scarecrow, he deterred
Any old kind of beastly bird,
With many types of crafty boxes
Set to entrap and kill the foxes,
And lots of evil-smelling tat
To scare away each dog and cat.
Wasn't it strange he was annoyed
To find his garden was a void.

Captain Sir Donald Swordfish's scarecrow

Yolande Spark

How should one view Yolande Spark,
Who sowed some turnips for a lark?
For she had somehow mixed the seeds,
So first came parsnips, then some swedes;
All her allotment thus was tangled
And all her wurzels truly mangled.

Within her plot at Ashton-under-Lyme
Portia Pumphrey thought to sow some thyme,
Considering this fairly harmless herb
Would not her many other plants disturb.
No sooner had the herb grown up, but why!
It vanished without trace into the sky.
Which really should have caused her no surprise,
Since everyone's aware of how thyme flies.

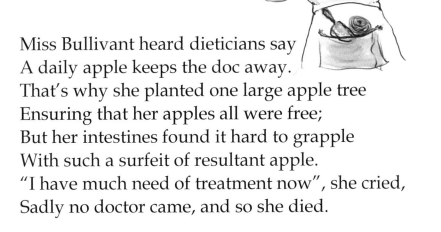

Miss Bullivant heard dieticians say
A daily apple keeps the doc away.
That's why she planted one large apple tree
Ensuring that her apples all were free;
But her intestines found it hard to grapple
With such a surfeit of resultant apple.
"I have much need of treatment now", she cried,
Sadly no doctor came, and so she died.

Algernon Pinkerton Codrington said
All his tomatoes would ripen to red;
Thus it was clear that he wasn't too keen
Finding the fruit stayed an obstinate green.
So, just to prove he could be just as fickle,
Algernon turned the offenders to pickle.

Mr Nathaniel Emerson Pomfret Grey
Grew marrows in a most determined way,
With all the art a gardener espouses
He nurtured them till they were big as houses.
With boastful pride this fellow then insisted
That every one of them be Grade One listed.
But then he kept them growing on, despite
The way they all increased in breadth and height.
Thus it was brought to Mr Grey's attention
That each was an unauthorised extension.
The sad result was that he was imprisoned,
And all his marrows very soon were wizened.

Jean de la Porte, though somewhat faddish,
Was really rather fond of radish;
And so he planted several rows,
Consuming all the best of those,
Though finding that he'd hardly started
When with a great aplomb he farted.

Jean de la Porte

Chas Claverton had heard that fish and chips
When served with mushy peas would please the lips
Of guests at supper, so it was hell-bent
To buy some, to the garden shop he went.
Seeing some packets clearly marked 'Sweet Peas',
He bought and quickly planted them, with ease.
Sad to relate, but when shove came to push
The flowers proved impossible to mush.

Enthused by a trip to Iberia,
June Medalsome planted wisteria.
But the length of its arms
Far exceeded its charms,
And reduced poor old June to hysteria

Old Sam

Old Sam, the gardener at Beauchamp Hall,
Espaliered a fruit tree on a wall;
Determined that his project would not fail,
He fastened it with tack and screw and nail.
It's sad but true that, after years elapsed,
The fruit tree prospered, but the wall collapsed.

Judge Enderby de Franck had heard that carrots
Should really be the food of choice for parrots,
Of which he had a pair, both red and green,
Which won big prizes on the parrot scene.
So you must pity this judicial fellow
When both his birds turned well and truly yellow.

Judge Enderby de Franck

When reading of the very strict embargo
On imports of all types of French escargots,
Jack Mainwaring, who owned a third of Wales,
Thought he might profit by producing snails.
The molluscs multiplied, and soon were seen
Devouring anything remotely green;
Once emerald as Ireland's Connemara,
Jack's acres now resembled the Sahara.
Much worse, Jack found what seemed to him incredible -
The snails he'd grown were totally inedible.

Jack Mainwaring's snails

Irwin von Braunsteiger

Irwin von Braunsteiger planted some figs,
Which he believed he could feed to his pigs.
Oddly, the swine took a shine to the stuff,
So that poor Irwin had not quite enough;
Thus the appalling result of all that -
His kraut was quite sauer, his wurst was all brat.

Snapdragons, mused Pat Horniman, were fun,
She sowed them, then transplanted every one,
Giving them loads of fertiliser feed,
Until the plants grew very large indeed;
So large, in fact, that, as she'd not assumed,
One opened - and poor Pat was quite consumed.

Sir Harry Herbivore thought beet
Could quickly turn to something sweet;
And so he pounded them to pulp
To stir with tea, but with one gulp
His sweet tooth was not pleased, instead
Sir Harry's face was turned bright red.

Hector McQuaid had heard that growing chives
Served to enhance the upper classes' lives,
Enabling him his pantry-maid to chivvy,
Disparaging the underpaid young skivvy.
Sadly, her boxer boyfriend could protect her
With blows upon the nose of poor old Hector.

Hector McQuaid

Claudia Towcester

Claudia Towcester cried "I can't
Enjoy success with any plant."
So she abandoned sowing seeds
And left her garden to the weeds;
But she was soon put on her mettle,
Encountering a giant nettle;
For so enormous was its sting
That there occurred the saddest thing;
Poor Claudia swelled into a ball,
Which didn't suit the girl at all.

Monsignor Michael Macready
Tried to comfort the poor and the needy;
So he gave them some hints
On the growing of mints,
An approach they considered quite seedy.

When Daisy Dungeon thought to prune her roses,
What she had first in mind was making posies.
What she forgot, however, were the thorns,
Sharper than those of any beast with horns.
Thus, little Daisy's body bled and bled,
And all the midges queued up to be fed.

Aloyius

Some men he knew persuaded Aloysius
That fully buttered parsnips were delicious;
And so he sowed some seeds, with gentle patting,
And, like Prince Charles, encouraged them with chatting.
Sad to relate, no matter what he uttered,
The parsnips obstinately stayed unbuttered.

Miss Mary Marjoribanks once decided
(though the thought was much derided)
Strong potato growth requires
A tower of ascending tyres.
The spuds then grew not smooth; instead
Each bore a well-embedded tread.

Miss Mary Marjoribanks

Reverend Tom

Reverend Tom believed that growing chilli
Would keep him cool in summer - which was silly.
He put them in a lovely sunny spot,
And prayed for providential aid a lot.
Sadly for Tom, his faith was soon eroded -
He swallowed just the one and then exploded.

Mr Rejoinder seemed to think
Gardenias should all be pink;
But when he found it was untrue,
As some appeared that were quite blue,
He flew into a rage, and said
"I'll have some yellow ones instead."

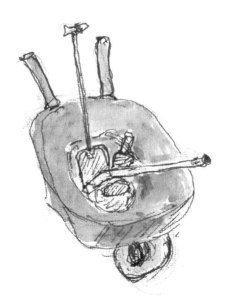

Mr Rejoinder

Clarence

Clarence thought consuming cauliflower
Would give him loads of pugilistic power;
And so he grew it, but collapsed in tears,
When it produced his cauliflower ears.

Madame Labelle loved fancy food to eat,
And so she grew some medlars for a treat.
When friends enquired why she had chosen medlars,
She said "It's just to keep away the pedlars."
"Illogical at best", said those she knew,
But Madame really knew a thing or two;
As a direct result of medlars meddling
Apparently the pedlars ceased their peddling.
Which goes to show that those who are astute
Keep very careful eyes upon their fruit.

Miss Enid Featherstonehaugh

Miss Enid Featherstonehaugh thought that she would fix
Her sweet peas to her grandpa's walking sticks.
She tied them up with raffia in bows
And watered them with care and with her hose.
So you may well imagine her dismay
When the ungrateful things just walked away.

The Earl of Crampton grew a prize cucumber
To win the garden show at Little Slumber.
It was so large his minion said "I'm sorry,
But, my Lord, we'll have to hire a lorry."
The transport thus arranged, this massive, posh,
Entitled salad item caused a squash.
Manoeuvred by a crane into the tent,
It banged into the central pole, and sent
The whole caboodle crashing to the ground,
Leaving the Earl's cucumber quite uncrowned.
The only winner was the lady who
Made picnics for a cricket team she knew.
Her very simple culinary reason
Was she'd have sandwich fillings for a season.

The Earl of Crampton's Cucumber

Miss Murk

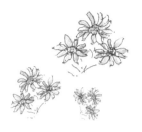

Miss Murk decided she would make
A hedge so thick it was opaque.
It was so tall, and also wide,
That nobody could see inside;
Finally, it was as they feared;
Miss Murk had simply disappeared.